A Splendid Isolation

A
Splendid
Isolation

———

Lessons on Happiness
from the
Kingdom of Bhutan

———

MADELINE DREXLER

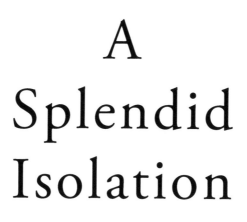

Cover photograph: Yangthang at sunrise, Haa district, Bhutan
Copyright © 2014 by Madeline Drexler

End page photograph: National Institute for Zorig Chusum (Traditional Arts and Crafts), Thimphu
Copyright © 2014 by Madeline Drexler

Back cover: Emblem of the Kingdom of Bhutan

First Print Edition: May 2014

ISBN-13: 978-1499362640
ISBN-10: 1499362641

www.madelinedrexler.com

A Splendid Isolation

1

གཅིག་

On Friday evenings in Thimphu, the capital of Bhutan, men, women, and children throng the main street, flowing together in a slow dance. Swaggering teenage boys, arms slung over each other's shoulders, speak in surprisingly gentle voices. Stray dogs assertively cohabit the city. One often hears singing— on sidewalks, pouring out of windows, on construction sites. The melodies persist in the undulating countryside, where men engaged in matches of archery or darts break into congratulatory chants when the other side scores. At Buddha Point, a bamboo guardrail catches the wind and makes the haunting flutter of a tenor recorder.

Article 9 of Bhutan's constitution says: "The State shall strive to promote those circumstances that will enable the successful pursuit of Gross National Happiness." In the fall of 2012, I traveled to this simple, complicated, lavishly lovely place to find out how GNH, as the policy is known, plays out in real life—or at least, that was my stated mission. The truth is, I had been drawn to Bhutan since my college days, when I read a small squib in a newspaper stating that the country permitted only 2,500 tourists a year. Now, more than three decades later, I recorded interviews with dozens of people, from scholars and lawmakers to activists and artists, and took notes on casual conversations in cities and villages, homes and monasteries, restaurants and cars. My intention was to glean what makes for happiness in a fast-changing society where Buddhism is deeply rooted but where the temptations and collateral damage of affluence are rising. Deep down, like anyone, I was curious about what makes for happiness, period.

A relentless self-help literature in the West caters to the same hunger: *The How of Happiness, Authentic Happiness, Stumbling on Happiness, The Happiness Solution, The Happiness Makeover, Happiness Now, Happiness Is a Choice, Happy Money.* Bhutan's GNH perspective turns this solo orientation upside down. It emphasizes not the individual but the collective, and how government can create the "enabling conditions" for people and society—they cannot be separated— to be happy. When I asked each of my interviewees what made them happy, their answers tended to the prosaic: their families, their friends, their hobbies. But when I asked what makes one happy—what makes for happiness in principle, what is worth aspiring to—the conversations caught fire.

Bhutanese have practiced happiness, reflected upon it, debated it, dissected it, and legislated it—and they seemed to me, on the whole, happier than Americans, at least for the time being. In Bhutan, I discovered that the act of contemplating happiness made me happy. My 22 days there were among the sweetest I have ever spent.

2

Sandwiched between the world's two most populous countries, India and China, Bhutan is half the size of Indiana, has a population of about 740,000, and has never been colonized. The land rises from 300 feet in the southern lowlands to more than 24,000 feet in the mountains—some sacred and unclimbed—bordering the Tibet Autonomous Region. (Since 2004, mountaineering has been banned here, in part out of deference to the belief that the peaks house protective deities.) Bhutan's constitution stipulates that 60 percent of the country must remain under forest cover forever; today, despite breakneck urbanization, that figure is 80 percent, and on the tiny international tarmac in Paro, flanked by forest and red rice paddies, the first sensory note after you step off the plane is the scent of wood. The government bans plastic bags. Capital punishment was abolished in 2004.

Bhutan is the only country in the world where Vajrayana Buddhism—deity-dense, merit-based, karma-focused—is the official religion. It is the only country in the world where Dzongkha—the soft, sibilant tongue closely related to Tibetan—is the national language. It is the only country in the world where the ngultrum—the official currency, handsomely printed—has buying power.

The national dish is hot chilies and cheese. The four most common household assets are a rice cooker, a curry cooker, a water boiler, and a religious altar. In government offices (and most other places) men wear the traditional *gho* (a cinched, knee-length, bathrobe-like garment that my women friends covet) with black knee socks (Gold Toe is the desired brand); women wear the traditional *kira* (a full-length dress or skirt-and-jacket combination with impossibly intricate pleats and folds). Prayer flags of mourning and celebration, delicately planted on every mountainside, are a visual throughline.

Bhutan prohibits tobacco advertising, smoking in public places, and the sale or illegal possession of tobacco products (but there was a public outcry in 2011 when a 23-year-old monk received a three-year jail sentence for smuggling in $2.50

worth of chewing tobacco). Government leaders have vowed to grow 100 percent organic crops (but most agricultural products are imported from India). National policy protects wildlife (but as a result, farmers often stay up all night, suffering sleep deprivation, to protect their fields from marauding elephants, wild pigs, and ravenous monkeys—a knotty issue known as "human-wildlife conflict"). The government seeks economic development (but offers few incentives for small, self-owned businesses—which are culturally perceived as ungenerous toward the collective). Bhutan has strict seat belt and anti-litter laws (but most citizens flout them). Homosexuality is illegal (but no one is arrested).

Like every country, Bhutan is rich in contradictions. Unlike most countries, its particular contradictions tend to draw idealists, who project their own struggles about how to live a genuine and ethical life writ large in this earnest, high-minded, increasingly self-confronting culture. The Bhutanese have not necessarily found the answers, but they are asking original questions.

3

གསུམ་

The Dzongkha language has few abstract words. One of them is the government's made-up term for GNH-style happiness: *Gakid Pelzom*. *Ga* means "happy," *kid* means peaceful, and *Gakid* conjoins the two into a single entity. *Pelzom* is a more complicated amalgam, with *pel* meaning wealth and prosperity, and *zom* convergence. In this linguistic alchemy, *Gakid Pelzom* connotes the holistic union of happiness, peace, and prosperity—"having it all," Vajrayana-style.

In Bhutan, every conversation about GNH became at some point definitional. Can a nation be happy if individuals are not? Can individuals be happy if others suffer? Will the country's traditional foundations of happiness erode, to be replaced by a surfeit of stuff? Bhutan's national policy flushes those questions out of the realms of mental reverie and into practicality.

At a dinner party, a professional woman joked, "Before, if someone asked if you were happy, you'd smile and say, 'Yes.' Now you say, 'What do you *mean*?'"

What *do* they mean?

In the capital, many told me, happiness is increasingly being defined as consumerism. "People in Thimphu are getting competitive. If he has a house, I want a house. If he has a car, I want a car," a young Ministry of Health worker told me. "The ones who are making money think GNH is good. The ones who aren't think GNH is bad. Making money is all people care about. I don't think GNH can work in Thimphu."

In rural Bhutan, older villagers' definition of happiness is starkly different. On the way to Punakha Dzong, the resplendent seventeenth-century monastery/fortress, I spoke (through a translator) with 79-year-old Sangay Lham, a smiling, gray-haired woman dressed in a checkered *kira* and fine silver broach, selling fruit by the side of the road. What, I asked, does GNH mean to her? "As long as we have fire when we need it, water when we need it, warm food on the table, tasty curry, what else do we need?" she said. "Be kind to everyone. Feed all the animals. Happiness is to be good at heart—and with the heart, a little wealth."

In this devoutly religious nation, the Buddhist conception
of happiness is pervasive. "We talk about the economy, but
the core Buddhist understanding of GNH, the reality of GNH
here, is the realization of compassion," said Lama Ngodup
Dorji, a man with a beatific face who is the seventeenth
member of his family over 15 generations to head the Shingkhar
Dechenling monastery. I met him in Thimphu at the offices of
the affiliated Ati Foundation, which gives economic assistance
to poor citizens and rural communities. The foundation is
housed in a brand-new glass-clad building with polished
marble floors and an Italian restaurant on the second floor.
The weather had turned chilly, and Dorji was wearing a down
vest over his red robes. Happiness, he said, warming his hands
around a fresh cup of coffee, is a choice. "You have to brew it
in yourself. Even from a lump of food, we choose each grain
to suit our need. Likewise, in the philosophical manner, we
choose to be who we are."

In my quest to define happiness in the land of GNH, I
also sought out Chencho Dorji (a shortlist of about 50 names
with religious meanings is endlessly recycled here, regardless of
gender). He was Bhutan's first psychiatrist; today there are
two. Dorji is a friendly and passionately voluble man with a
brush cut and mustache. He entered the profession in the late
1980s, when he could not find proper care for his older
brother, a monk who had suffered a breakdown and become
violently schizophrenic. I visited Dorji in his tiny office at the
JDW National Referral Hospital, the nation's largest medical
facility, in Thimphu. With its long queues and dim, echoing
hallways, the hospital has, to American senses, the ambience of
a Greyhound bus station.

Western psychiatry, like Western culture, focuses on

individual neuroses, Dorji told me. But in Bhutan, happiness is grounded in the belief that everyone's innate nature is peaceful, and that unhappiness springs from estrangement from that nature—another way of stating the Buddhist idea that liberation, or the "unconditioned" state, follows relinquishment of the enslaving conditions of our minds and bodies. As a psychiatrist and a Buddhist, Dorji bridges Western and Eastern traditions. "The true, natural mind is like the moon or the sun—it's clear and radiant and graceful and majestic. Our perceptions, emotions, all our predispositions are like clouds," he said. "Those clouds are the 'appearance' mind. I'm treating a thought disorder, an emotional disorder, a perceptual disorder such as auditory hallucinations—to me, these are all 'appearance mind.' It's not the true mind. That's where we have a difference with the West. When we say GNH, we are saying we want to get closer to our natural mind."

GNH, he added, is intended to support the naturally contented mind. But the policy is not foolproof. "Even the Buddha could not decide who would be happy or not. He just showed the way."

4

"What is ironic is that happiness is what everybody desires, and yet it is something that everybody trivializes," Bhutan's first democratically elected prime minister, Jigme Y. Thinley, told me. (In an election upset, he and his ruling Peace and Prosperity party— Druk Phuensum Tshogpa, or DPT—were voted out in July 2013, in part because of the country's decline in that second P.) Thinley is a compact, fine-featured man with high cheekbones, almond eyes, and a felt-lined voice with a slightly raspy edge. We spoke in a bright and spacious office with creamy yellow walls, gleaming pine floors, and over the fireplace, as in every public space, a large photo of the dashing young king. Outside, white-walled Tashichho Dzong, the seat of Bhutan's civil government, was blinding in the sun.

Thinley has been Bhutan's most avid and eloquent salesman for Gross National Happiness. "What is happiness as we have defined here in Bhutan?" he said. "Happiness is a state of being in which the needs of the body and the mind are equally met within a peaceful and stable environment." GNH, he said, was designed as an antidote to the vulnerability we humans suffer because of insatiable greed (he was invoking the three mental toxins in Buddhism, the other two being hatred and delusion). "The material world has developed such means, such powerful instruments, to feed that greed."

To put this countercultural rhetoric in context, it helps to know Bhutan's recent history. If the word "materialism" is earnestly bruited about here, much as it was in America during the 1960s, it's largely because, until quite recently, Bhutan was a medieval society (serfdom was abolished in 1956). In 1959, when Tibetans staged an uprising against Communist Chinese occupation and were brutally suppressed, Bhutan's Third King, Jigme Dorji Wangchuck, apprehended that Bhutan, now vulnerable to Chinese incursion, could no longer go it alone. So began a cautious policy of opening to the outside world, as well as a strong Bhutan alignment with India that continues to this day.

At the time, virtually the entire nation was rural.

Thimphu, a collection of peasant hamlets situated in a valley on the banks of the Wang Chu river, became the official capital only in 1961. Average life expectancy was 33 years. The gross national product per person was $51. There was no centralized government administration. Agriculture was subsistence—people bred animals and cultivated only as much from the land as they needed. They wove their own cloth for traditional garments and made their own pottery. There were no roads and no motor vehicles—mules, yaks, and horses were the principal modes of transport. There was no electricity, no telecommunications network, and no postal system. Foreign visitors were not permitted. (In 1974, the first year travel restrictions were eased, the government issued 287 visas.) Bhutan had only four hospitals and two qualified doctors. An informal public health metric for physical exercise was the diameter of men's (and presumably women's) calves, and a familiar saying was, "Your calf is so big, it can dam a river."

Then, under the Third King, everything started to change. The first paved road was completed in 1962. Schools and hospitals were built. Citizens gained free health care and free education. Beginning in primary grades, English became the language of instruction in all public schools, with Dzongkha taught as the national language. Larger-scale agriculture and industry emerged. Safe drinking water and electricity became priorities. Polio was eliminated in 1986, leprosy in 1990, goiter (from lack of dietary iodine) in 2003. Internet and a national TV station arrived in 1999. Today, life expectancy stands at 67.6 years. The childhood immunization rate is upwards of 93 percent. Eighty-six percent of people ages 15 to 24 are literate. Per capita income is just under $3,000. More than 100,000 tourists visited the country in 2012. Ninety-three percent of households own a cell phone. About a third of the population is urban, and the government predicts that figure could rise to 70 percent by 2020. Men's calves have shrunk.

Of course, with development have come problems. Urbanization has put a strain on housing and sanitation. The issue of domestic violence has entered public discourse. The Indian rupee—the main currency for trade—is in short supply, and the country's own currency has tumbled in value. The economy is stagnant, the private sector is on the verge of collapse, and inflation is soaring. Youth unemployment is up, and along with it formerly rare violations such as drug abuse and vandalism. In Thimphu, there are 700 bars and one public library. The country struggles with a dire shortage of doctors and nurses. When a recent government survey asked respondents how their welfare could be most improved, their top answers reflected the stubborn needs of a developing nation, GNH or not: roads, water, commerce, transportation, and communications.

One afternoon, I spoke, through a translator, with Dorji Gyeltshen, a 70-year-old man roasting maize by the side of the road. "I feel like I've lived three lives," he said wearily—meaning life in isolated Bhutan, life in the nascent GNH era, and life today, where anything goes, or so it seems, including pale Western visitors plying him with questions. "When tourists come to Bhutan and see us in Western clothes, it's not a good sight," he said. "If I get an audience with the king, I'd like to bring up this point."

In Bhutan, which is ranked 140 of 186 countries in the 2012 UN Human Development Index, the operative question is how this nation can become materially modern without losing its soul.

5

ཉ.

Looking out my hotel window one night, this is what I saw: dark clouds skimming a half moon; the orange-pink lighted dome of Memorial Chorten—the most visible religious ← landmark in Bhutan, built to honor the Third King—floating above the city; teenagers in twos and threes and fours, striding toward Clock Tower Square; in the bedraggled office building across the street, a giant faded photo of the young king and queen, and signs for Wangthang Computer World and Prime Infotech and Guru Consultancy Services; directly below, an old woman bent over the sidewalk, attentively making her way with a small hand broom. This is what I heard: rising and fading choruses of stray dogs; an American-style band undertaking "Born to Be Wild" and "Knocking on Heaven's Door" to hoots and shouts from the crowd. This is what I smelled: burning incense and the faint cedary whiff of *doma,* the stimulating, red-stained, pervasively expectorated chew of betel nuts and lime paste wrapped in betel leaves.

I was completely content. But Thimphu had taken getting used to. I had expected to find the familiar trappings of a city, where I would be in the thick of the action. My first impressions were so deflating that I wondered whether I had made a mistake by booking a cheap, centrally located hotel for three weeks.

Guidebooks never fail to mention that in the early 1990s Thimphu authorities installed the city's first traffic light at a bustling intersection, but the technological intrusion was so jarring, they removed it, returning to the white-gloved policeman or -woman in a little raised gazebo who artistically directs traffic and toots a whistle when schoolkids jaywalk. Every building hews to a traditional exterior design—no more than six stories high, all stucco and timber, fancifully painted—that creates a satisfying harmony for the eye. No auteurist architectural statements here. Even the gas stations are charming.

What most forcefully struck me, however, was the proliferation of new construction sites, each wrapped in a rickety nest of bamboo scaffolding. Vertical stands of dark rusted rebar on the roofs inversely echoed the spectral stands of white prayer flags on the encircling mountains. Thimphu has no apparent city plan. Lean, acrobatic workers perch unsecured on narrow planks, wielding crude tools: metal hammerheads shoved into wooden handles, simple handsaws. The only sign of industrialization are small cement mixers, spewing fumes. In part because of its topsy-turvy growth, the nation has suffered a "rupee crunch": the supply of Indian rupees has not kept up with demand, a complicated situation driven by a surge of capital expenditures, banks making too many private loans without determining if people could pay back, and Bhutan's utter dependence on imports from India.

One can't escape a sense of development spinning out of control, in plain sight. But the Bhutanese embrace what an American might consider a casual attitude toward risk. In a place where natural hazards abound, they accept manmade hazards of all sorts. This nonchalance is apparent on Bhutan's famously tortuous roads. In many cars and trucks, wooden phalluses dangle from rear-view mirrors to keep away evil spirits. Yet road injuries, often linked to alcohol (liver disease caused by drinking is the top killer here), are a major cause of death in Bhutan. "Drinking whisky, Driving risky," reads one sign. "If you are married, divorce speed," admonishes another.

Late one afternoon, winding along a mountain road to the capital, my driver Tandin, who is skilled and cautious at the wheel, glanced into his rear-view mirror and gave a start. I looked around. A truck had veered off the road and its white cab was enmeshed in the treetops below. We were quiet for a few minutes. Hesitantly, I suggested to Tandin that he might think about wearing a seat belt. He smiled and shook his head. "I am not comfortable with it," he said. Bhutanese believe that seat belts increase danger, by trapping people who would otherwise—somehow, miraculously—escape from free-falling vehicles. In this GNH nation, magical thinking is not limited to highway safety.

6

དྲུག

Bhutan's political leaders are keen to stress that Gross National Happiness is not a Buddhist idea; it harmonizes, they say, with all religions. But traveling through Bhutan, I found it difficult to disentangle Bhutanese culture from Buddhism, and I became convinced that GNH could only have sprung up in Buddhist soil.

The prayer flags that stitch the landscape together—spectral white with black inscriptions for the dead, primary colors for happy occasions—are merely the most obvious sign of this pervasive devotion. Vajrayana Buddhism, which is common in Bhutan, Tibet, and Nepal, rests on the reciting of mantras and on the worship of mountains, lakes, and often terrifying deities believed to subdue evil spirits. It's a kind of fast lane to enlightenment, compared to the slow lane of rigorous self-examination in Theravada Buddhism, the original form preached by the Buddha. And there is a spiritual hierarchy of prayers: some for oneself (the lowest form); some for people one knows (intermediate); and some for all sentient beings, a devotional catchment that includes humans and animals. "Gross" in the sense of "aggregate" or "collective" resides deep in the Bhutanese psyche.

"The greatest religion gives suffering to nobody," reads a weather-beaten sign, quoting the Buddha, at Chele La pass, the highest motorable point in the country, near Paro. This maxim is everywhere evident. As a Bhutanese friend and I walked in the mountains one afternoon, he reflexively removed insects from the path and gently placed them in the verge, out of harm's way. Early one morning in Thimphu, I saw a group of young schoolboys, in their spotless white-sleeved *ghos*, crouching over a mouse on the street, gently offering it food. In Bhutan, the horses that trudge up the steep trail to the Tiger's Nest monastery are reserved for out-of-shape tourists; Bhutanese don't consider horses beasts of burden and prefer not to make them suffer under heavy loads. Even harvesting honey is considered a sign of disrespect for the industrious bees; my young guide, Kezang, admonished me for buying a bottle of Bhutanese honey to take home. (Chastened, I left it there.)

In a popular book titled *Mindful Living in Bhutan,* the influential monk Khenpo Phuntsok Tashi explains that the deep, unbounded connections between all living things can be experienced through compassion, a central concept in Vajrayana

Buddhism: "Compassion is the genuine attitude that opens up everything, it is not a practice of self-contained meditation or self-enlightenment, it is a practice of making more space for every sentient being."

To illustrate, he describes a meditation with bracing imagery straight out of the Himalayas: "A good exercise would be if you think of a yak, for example, being taken from the high mountains to a lower place and then to a market for slaughter. First it is dragged from its herd and experiences paralyzing fear. Next, it is thrown on its back and the feet are bound together while a muzzle is tightly applied which binds its nose and face and creates a feeling of suffocation as the animal begins to die. Hardly has death passed over the animal when the body is subject to knives, which slice and skin and cut the once-living body into many small parts.

"Continue with this exercise by moving from thinking of this poor creature as just a yak and instead think of the animal as your very own mother. Ask yourself sincerely what would you do? When you experience in the depth of your heart your motivation to prevent your mother from being tortured and slaughtered in such a horrific way, reflect that although this suffering creature is not actually your mother in this life, it could have been a parent at sometime in a previous life. This will assist you in understanding the importance of compassion being provided to all."

In Bhutan I encountered an extravagant sense of generosity. At the annual masked dances that are a major tourist draw in late September in the capital, worshipers from across the country were dressed in their finest attire: women in silk *kiras*, men in *ghos* set off by broad silk scarves, called *kabneys,* draped from the left shoulder to the right hip. In the vast courtyard of Tashichho Dzong, a broiling sun beat down on the spectators, who squeezed into every available space and oozed forward every time someone left. Heads were covered with colorful handkerchiefs. I hadn't brought water, and there was no food or drink on the religious grounds. Having been unwell the day before, I now felt faint and worried how I could extricate myself from the crowd. Suddenly a creased hand appeared in front of my face: an old woman was offering me a fat, juicy slice of cucumber. She gave me a *doma*-stained smile. "It's fresh," she said, in English. Never so ravenous for cucumber, I survived the afternoon.

Such compassion begins in the family, and love of family is paramount. "Is it true that it is the custom in America that children should move away from their parents?" Kezang asked me, in a tone of moralistic disbelief. She is in her early twenties, and wherever we went together, young men would smile and make flirtatious banter, to which Kezang was unresponsive. Once, I asked her to describe her ideal mate. She said, "Someone who loves my parents as much as I do."

Compassion flows out to the Bhutanese people and country. At Punakha Dzong, which houses the remains of Shabdrung Ngawang Namgyal, the Tibetan Buddhist lama who unified the warring fiefdoms of Bhutan into a nation state, I met a friendly, red-robed monk named Kesang. I asked how he thought GNH was playing out. "Our kingdom is blooming year by year," he said with a grin. "The government is doing everything for us, and every year it is getting better and better. It's not because of GNH. Since the time Shabdrung has been here, we have had GNH."

In Bhutan, I had expected to get living instruction in the Eightfold Path. Since 2000, I have avidly studied and practiced Buddhism—the unembellished, self-investigating, Theravada strain that was seeded in the United States in the 1970s. But in a country suffused with Buddhism, I was surprised to discover that many of my acquaintances had never formally studied the religion and didn't consider themselves particularly pious. One friend—the insect rescuer—apologetically explained that Buddhism "is just in my genes." And in an e-mail exchange shortly before my trip, I had expressed gratitude to an extraordinarily helpful contact. In my delusion of a common spiritual language, I wrote that he embodied the first of the ten Buddhist *paramis,* or perfections: *dana,* or generosity. "Haha," he replied. "I am clueless about Buddhism."

Not everyone here claims to be clueless. One morning in early October, I visited the Centre for Bhutan Studies, where the boundary between indoors and outdoors is purposely blurred. The center's president, Dasho Karma Ura, planted 2,000 trees on the property when he founded it in 1999. The unheated wood-paneled office has big windows that look out into forest—an expanse of green that vibrated with stridulating crickets.

GNH aficionados abroad admire Ura for his scholarly framing of Bhutan's vision—a vision embedded in Buddhism. He has an austere presence: closely trimmed, slightly receding hair, wire-rimmed glasses, contained movements. Though he seldom looked at me while we were talking—instead gazing to the side and declaiming, as if in a school oratory competition— he spoke in a beautiful, sometimes mischievous soliloquy: an impromptu lecture on dharma.

When we first sat down, I mentioned that his office seems to invite the forest indoors. "I refuse to build," he said proudly, looking out the windows. "The government spends so much money on building. They express themselves through structures. It's one of the necessary notions of modernization and development: buildings." Ura designed the center's headquarters not to last. "It will disintegrate and leave no trace. It has no foundation. It's standing on blocks of stones. For me, light, color, trees are far more important than inanimate things around you. . . . All of us must reflect on our life as a traveler— sixty, seventy years. . . . One must feel impermanence all the time, and buildings are an obstruction to that feeling."

As he spoke, I couldn't help thinking about Bhutan's 2011 earthquake. A few days earlier, on a trip to the western district of Haa, I had seen health clinics and homes riddled with cracks. Was Ura's paean to architectural transience really what a citifying GNH society needed?

He steered our conversation over heady topics: the necessity of antimarket forces in a society newly enchanted with consumer goods, the unpredictability of democracy, the spiritual benefits of moderate physical labor, the gloominess of impersonal cities, the reflective conversation of rural people, the dangers of sensory overload. When a large bee entered the room, Ura reached into his *gho* and slipped out a white handkerchief. In a swift gesture he captured the visitor, calmly walked to the front door, and set it free.

7

One of the first things that strikes a visitor in Bhutan is the stray dog population. Tourist guides warn travelers not to take a room in the center of Thimphu because of the nightly howling of the packs. I intentionally took a room in the center of town and enjoyed the nocturnal concerts. Thimphu has upwards of 5,000 stray dogs.

The Buddhist reverence for all life is one reason strays have survived here. In the cycle of rebirths, dogs are believed to be the last reincarnation before humans, and people often put out leftovers for the animals for a good rebirth. But the scheme of rebirth also holds that a dog suffers because of its own bad karma. In the land of the Thunder Dragon, a dog's life is therefore precarious.

Since 1997, a Frenchwoman named Marianne Guillet, who grew up in Normandy, has rescued more than 50,000 stray dogs. One afternoon, I visited Guillet and her Dutch partner, a civil engineer named Hendrik Visser, at the Pilou Medical Center, a nonprofit animal rescue and rehabilitation clinic in the Yusupang section of Thimphu, high in the surrounding hills. They live frugally off Visser's salary and scant donations, and they take no vacations.

When the couple arrived in Bhutan, dogs were starving and dying in the streets, often with open and bleeding wounds. Today, Guillet's charges are marginally healthier but frequently malnourished. They suffer skin diseases such as mange and scabies. And just as the Bhutanese people are being buffeted by modernization, dogs too are vulnerable to cultural and environmental change. As car and truck traffic increases, for example, so does the number of injured animals, who for centuries have been accustomed to sleeping undisturbed on dirt roads. Guillet nurtures the animals back to health, sterilizes them, and tattoos a number in their ears, in case they turn up at Pilou again (many do).

On the day I visited, there were about 150 dogs, 20 macaques, and 15 cats on the premises, a happy chaos. (Guillet has also rescued ferrets, goats, birds, deer, pigs, rats, and snakes.) Some of the animals lived in large fenced compounds, others roamed the grounds. As we talked on the porch, a rescued tabby kitten crawled up my pants leg and curled up in my lap, while a black puppy gnawed on my shoelaces. It is a supremely egalitarian environment. The prime minister's Pekingese, Sintu—who was there for minor surgery—cavorted with recovering strays off the street. "Everybody here gets the royal treatment," Guillet joked.

Guillet describes herself as "a Buddhist with Judeo-Christian genetics." She is bracing and one-off, a robust woman with direct, soulful eyes and hurtling speech. "For me, the truth is so simple—and I mean, it's *very* simple. I just know that the teaching of Buddha—not the dogmatic Buddhism, not the ritual, but the scientific way or the philosophy of Buddhism—is the truth," she said. "Everything is an illusion. I create my own suffering. But the suffering of those animals is not an illusion: They suffer."

I asked Guillet about her upbringing. "You know the family jokes that everybody says at each birthday party? For me, since I was one year old, it was how I saved the mosquito in the water, how I would never eat a steak in my life, how I would punch kids in school when they were trying to kill bees or ants. The girl scouts would think it's funny to cut an insect in twos and threes. For me, that was a holocaust." As a child, Guillet taught herself how to repair cockroach legs and butterfly wings, using cotton buds, toothpicks, matches, absorbent paper, and glue.

We walked the grounds as the sun set over the green

mountains in a vibrant display and I asked Guillet one of my standard questions: Is she happy? "I would say no, I'm extremely unhappy. People are killing each other everywhere. Humanity has not had a big evolution in the last twenty-five thousand years, that I can see."

Pressing the issue, I asked what *did* make her happy. "I would say that what makes me happy is to understand things. There are always three truths: yours, mine, and *the* truth. If I can get closer to yours, it's interesting. If I can get closer to mine, it's liberating. And if I can get closer to *the,* it's enlightening."

In Bhutan, Guillet is known by the Dzongkha term *Rochi Ama*—"Dog Mother." (Having never wanted children, she prefers "friend" or "protector.") In 2008, she received the Coronation gold medal from the prime minister for her services to society. "In France, they would put me in a straitjacket. Here, they put me on a pedestal."

8

Bhutanese have many sayings about the anchoring spirit of home. "It is better to eat a bowl of porridge at home than to dine in a palace." "It is better to sleep under a bridge at home than to stay in a grand hotel." Underlying love of home is a fierce national pride, which may not be unique to Bhutan but does perhaps explain its claim of never having been colonized by another power and its vow to maintain tradition while raising living standards. "The sense of identity, the sense of being Bhutanese and of loving the country, is amazing," said the cultural historian Françoise Pommaret, an elegant woman with a short silver coif who, having lived in Bhutan for more than 30 years, has witnessed the country's modern transformation. "Bhutanese are resilient—laid-back, maybe, but resilient. And when it comes to their country, they are tough, tough, tough."

As in many developing countries and small tribal communities, the cherishing of home is reinforced by a thick social weave. Bhutan is a village that masquerades as a nation. I found it comical that virtually everyone with whom I had scheduled an interview personally knew everyone else with whom I had scheduled an interview: They were old friends, they worked together, they had gone to the same college, their kids attended the same school, or, most frequently, they were blood relatives. Dasho Karma Ura was Kezang's uncle. Bhutan's most famous singer, the divine Dechen Pem, was my driver Tandin's older sister.

The social web is also supple enough to hold outsiders. In no country have I felt less like a stranger. I had traveled there alone, but once my plane landed, I was almost never by myself. My cell phone constantly rang with calls from brand-new friends, asking how I was and did I need anything and could I come over for dinner that night. In the streets I was never followed by men (unlike my experience in India and Sri Lanka), but was nodded at and greeted with self-possessed smiles by men and women, boys and girls.

At the Ambient Café, a light-filled, wood-and-wicker gathering spot that caters to expatriates and their local contacts, the talk spilled over from one table to the next—so unlike American coffeehouses, where everyone is hunched over a laptop, ears plugged into a private music library. At the

Ambient, it would almost be rude to shut out others in this way. One corner held a newspaper rack and a book swap. A young man with a Mohawk and tattoos on each knuckle—still an unusual aesthetic here, though styles are changing—soon memorized my tea order and noticed when I wasn't there for a day or so. I would climb the stairs dutifully lugging my laptop to do some work, only to fall into unhurried conversation and leave with the work undone, yet somehow better prepared for the next interview. It was a classic "third place," neither home nor work, the kind of environment extolled by those who ponder civic engagement.

One day, Visser, the Dog Mother's partner, happened to walk in. He joined me at my table, made political chitchat, opened his laptop, and pulled up a quote he thought I'd like, from Jean Giono's book *The Man Who Planted Trees*: "Everyone searches desperately for happiness, but the price we must pay for it is generosity."

9

ད་ཐ་

When first conceived, Gross National Happiness was the enlightened guiding principle of development at a time when Bhutan was starting to emerge from cultural isolation and material deprivation. But the country's official pursuit of happiness was not new. Bhutan's 1729 legal code declared that "if the Government cannot create happiness for its people, there is no purpose for the Government to exist."

Since 1907, Bhutan had been ruled by a lineage of

progressive monarchs in the Wangchuck family. The most
visionary of these was the Fourth Dragon King, Jigme Singye
Wangchuck, who took the throne at 16 after his father's death
in 1972. Two years later, shortly after his coronation, he coined
the witty phrase Gross National Happiness.

Photos of Wangchuck show an almost somber man.
"He was mature beyond his years. He had an aura. He
commanded. We knew that what he was going to say was
wise. And he had been like that all his life. He cared for
people," said the king's cousin, Dasho Paljor Dorji, popularly
known as Dasho Benji, who founded Bhutan's Royal Society
for the Protection of Nature. The two men often traveled
together around the country, Benji serving as the monarch's
companion and chauffeur. "While the rest of us were hunting,
fishing, having fun, he was studying his people, talking to
them. What did they grow? What were their aspirations?
What did they want? What did they need? Everything he did
was in consultation with the people. As a young king, he
wanted to bring development into the country, but not at the
expense of our culture, our value system."

A 1987 story in Britain's *Financial Times* gave the
Fourth King an early international forum: "'We are convinced
that we must aim for contentment and happiness. Whether we
take five years or 10 to raise the per capita income and
increase prosperity is not going to guarantee that happiness
. . .' says King Jigme Singye Wangchuck, the country's 33-
year-old monarch, who puts gross national happiness above
targets of gross national product."

In late 2006, Wangchuck announced that he was
voluntarily giving up the throne to make way for a parliamentary
democracy in the form of a constitutional monarchy—perhaps

the only case in history in which an absolute monarch abdicated to make way for a peaceful transition to democracy. "In the Buddhist world, it is considered the ultimate sacrifice for a king," Pommaret told me. (Though the king is head of state, he is not the head of government. The prime minister—an elected official and head of the winning party—holds the position for a five-year term.)

The Fourth King's conception of Gross National Happiness rested on four "pillars": good governance, sustainable socioeconomic development, cultural preservation, and environmental conservation. This is the most concise summary of GNH—and many Bhutanese believe that further elaboration is unnecessary. Wangchuck's son, Jigme Khesar Namgyel Wangchuck, the current Fifth King, distilled the idea in a similarly pithy way in a 2009 speech: "To me it signifies simply Development with Values," he said, later adding, "Our government must be human."

The humanity of GNH is seen in the roomy definitions of what are known as the policy's nine "domains": good governance; psychological well-being; balanced time use; community vitality; health; education; culture; living standards; and ecological diversity and resilience. "Living standard" refers not merely to per capita income but also to meaningful work. "Environment" includes not only the measured quality of water, air, and soil but also how people perceive the quality of their natural surroundings. "Education" encompasses not just level of schooling, but also how involved parents are in their children's studies. "Community vitality" reflects not only crime but also volunteerism.

To get a clearer sense of how these ideas play out in policy, I visited Karma Tshiteem, secretary of Bhutan's Gross

National Happiness Commission. I had first met Tshiteem at an April 2012 United Nations conference on GNH. He sat at my lunch table and impressed me as a jokester and a sharp observer—the class cut-up who was also the smartest student. Now we were sitting over tea in a modestly furnished, glassed-in anteroom to his office. He wore a charcoal gray *gho* and carried on his right hip an incongruous ceremonial sword, a reminder of his responsibility to the people. It was dinnertime. Tshiteem looked tired and slightly rumpled from a day of back-to-back meetings, yet in typical Bhutanese fashion he was open and gracious, and never once glanced at his watch.

In gauging the happiness of Bhutanese, he told me: "We find that conventional parameters are far inadequate and are biased mainly to the material. . . . What is missing are the softer aspects. Psychological well-being is one. Another is community vitality, which is about recognizing human relationships as fundamental to meaning and happiness in life. Culture and tradition as fundamental to identity. And lastly, time use—that most precious of commodities, but one which we ignore when we are making development choices."

I asked Tshiteem if a GNH society was really possible, and mentioned that though smoking is illegal in Bhutan's public places, I had seen kids lighting up. "That's OK," he said. "There is no one ideal GNH human being. And we are not trying to define a GNH person. We posit GNH, but it doesn't mean we won't have these outliers and we will not have a problem with youth, because youth is a time of exploration and rebellion. GNH or no GNH, that can't change. That's human nature. GNH doesn't mean that everything has to be picture-perfect all the time."

In Bhutan, major policy proposals go through a GNH

screening tool—and this screening tool has teeth. In 2008, for example, GNH Commission officials were enthusiastic about joining the World Trade Organization. A preliminary vote showed 19–5 in favor of joining, based solely on economic criteria. But when the proposal was fed through the GNH policy-screening tool, which assesses draft policies based on their impact on GNH's nine domains, the downsides far outweighed the benefits. Among other things, WTO membership would have compelled the green-centric and health-conscious country to open its economy to a phalanx of junk food franchises such as McDonald's and Domino's Pizza. A second vote was taken, and the proposal lost 19–5. Bhutan did not join the WTO.

"What this tells us is that the decisions we make are very much influenced by the frameworks we use," said Tshiteem. "When you use the same framework that every other government uses, even Bhutanese arrive at the same conclusions. But when we brought in the GNH framework, which made them think deeply about all the other aspects that are important, suddenly they did not see this as such a great idea. One of the results from the screening tool was that WTO membership would raise the level of stress. That's something that would never be measured in the United States in anything having to do with economics."

Every two years, Bhutan conducts a fine-grained survey that captures the texture of citizens' interior lives. Among the revealing questions that you will never find in American government questionnaires: Do you consider Karma in the course of your daily life? Is lying justifiable? Do you feel like a stranger in your family? How much do you trust your neighbor? The survey asks respondents if they know the names of their great-grandparents; if eating too much fatty food is bad for health; if men make better leaders than women (gender equality is preached but not nearly achieved); if they planted trees in the past year; how they rate their total household income (in 2010, 71 percent said "just enough" and 20.3 percent said "more than enough"); if they think Bhutanese have become more concerned about material wealth (87.8 percent said yes); if they feel safe from ghosts ("rarely," 20 percent said).

Respondents are considered "happy" if they achieve "sufficiency" in at least six of the nine domains, not outsized achievement in one domain at the expense of another. As Tshiteem reminded me, in Buddhism, happiness is balance. Each of GNH's nine domains is "important on its own," he said. "You can't make up for lack of personal time with community vitality—you cannot. Because each domain, in itself, is a necessary condition. Sometimes we say, 'Look at these as nine wells. Our people should be able to drink deeply of all nine wells.'"

These are ambitious standards. In the 2010 survey, 40.8 percent of survey respondents in the land of Gross National Happiness tested happy. If Americans were surveyed on the same range of profound questions—culturally translated, of course—I suspect the outcome would be no better.

10

བཅུ་

One Sunday, Chencho Dorjee, a friend in public health, invited me to a *puja*, or religious ceremony, in a small temple his father-in-law had built in a tiny village called Gidakom, which stood high in the mountains between the valleys of Paro and Thimphu. Double rows of leafy birches and white prayer flags snapped in the stiff wind. Spreading down one valley were terraced plots of red rice, apple trees, carrots, chilies, and beans. An old leprosy hospital and a handful of houses occupied the other.

Inside the temple, from morning to sunset, elderly men and women and younger monks chanted and droned, fingered prayer beads, and spun their hand-held prayer wheels. But there was no solemn formality here. People wandered in and out. Dogs lounged around and peered inside. I was offered tea and food and holy water, and was encouraged to photograph and record the ceremony from any vantage point I wished. Perched cross-legged on a kind of plush daybed, the presiding monk—Chencho's brother-in-law—had the impassive, ironic face of a Jewish comedian.

Chencho's family shared their meals in a convivial circle on the floor of a stone kitchen with a single lightbulb dangling from the ceiling. As their guest, I was served lunch and dinner on a carpeted platform in a separate room, in the traditional style. (I yearned to join them.) The food was simple and hearty: eggs and cheese, a soup made of greens, rice and noodles, and the requisite milk tea, which simmered in a giant aluminum pot on an outdoor wood stove, constantly stirred by one or another family member. It was a "dry day"—meaning no meat or alcohol, which was consonant with Buddhist precepts and made the prayers more meaningful.

The wind in the valleys rose up in a bowl-like hum, punctuated by an unseen rushing stream. The trill and buzz of crickets and cicadas signaled the harvest season. Hours passed.

Sun and sharp shadows turned to blue twilight, and the air quickly cooled. With the dogs prancing around, the elderly villagers, who had eaten and prayed and slept alongside each other for six days, rolled up their bedding and pulled on their shoes and said goodbye to each other, shaking hands and laughing. For me, the scene felt familiar, like the exodus after a long dharma retreat in the U.S. Then the villagers and monks hopped into a small cordon of SUVs and trucks and drove off.

We were the last to leave—Chencho and I in the front seat of his Land Cruiser, his wife and sister and mother in back. By the front gate, wanly waving goodbye, looking disconsolate, was Karma, the presiding monk. "He will be lonely," said one of the women.

Darkness settled and a full moon rose above the lush mountains. Little lights flickered in the valley. "Thimphu is very beautiful," Chencho said. He turned on a CD: Leo Sayer's twangy early '80s hit, "More Than I Can Say," a song Chencho loved in college. The family sang along sleepily. Chencho played the track again, and again they sang along. That afternoon, I had told Chencho that I wanted to remember every sight and sound from this trip. He shrugged his shoulders and said, "Bhutanese just go from one moment to the next. They don't expend effort trying to record and recall. And therefore they probably forget a lot."

11

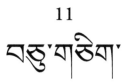

Tshering Tobgay—formerly Bhutan's opposition leader in Parliament, where I visited him, now prime minister—is a tall, strapping man with a shaved head whose physical energy is barely contained, even while seated. Soft-spoken, Harvard-educated, he at times steered our conversation in what felt more like a Socratic dialog than an interview, answering each of my queries with a broader question. At other times, he was bracingly candid. Unlike nearly everyone else I interviewed, over the customary tea and milk, this espresso lover served coffee with cream.

In American politics, Tobgay would probably be slotted as a libertarian brain with a communitarian heart. He heads the People's Democratic Party, which believes in smaller government, decentralized power, and a strong business sector. "What is a good society? What is a just society? There is no common definition," he told me. "Is meditation good? Yes. But can you impose that practice on others? Can you say that this is absolutely the best? A person would gain all the wonders of meditation by an early morning walk in the forest, or being a total atheist, or going for a morning jog, or gardening. Some people, with loud, head-banging music."

Tobgay observed that the Bhutanese were becoming more fractious under democracy. "We are very respectful of authority. It is not in our nature to criticize. We are also complacent politically, because we had everything given to us. That said, now many of the commentators in their blogs can be extremely direct. . . . Given the opportunity and the freedom of anonymity, we can get quite divisive. And this is in a society where political ideologies are not even well-defined."

Outside Bhutan, GNH enjoys great cachet in liberal circles, as dozens of cities and countries dip their toes in the philosophy. And with its tourist logo "Happiness Is a Place," Bhutan is a prized destination for spiritual-minded vacationers. I brought up Bhutan's star status among political progressives in the U.S., and recited an exchange I overheard on the trail to the Tiger's Nest monastery. An American tourist was sharply questioning her guide about the proliferation of polyester prayer flags, which take longer to biodegrade. The guide explained that polyester flags cost less. Unmollified, the tourist whined: "Where's the *soul*?"

To my surprise, Tobgay agreed with the righteous tourist. "We can't claim to the world to be GNH, whatever GNH means," he said, "if we don't want to make small sacrifices—cleaning up the mountainside, paying a bit more for your prayer flags. I am not saying polyester is wrong, but don't preach organic and use chemical."

Tobgay is equally skeptical about the Western left's glorification of Bhutan—"the people who tout and market Bhutan as a living Shangri-la." When I suggested that the Himalayan nation may be the political flavor of the month, he ruefully agreed. "Bhutan is small, nonthreatening. This can be very cute. And people who are frustrated are desperately looking for alternate paradigms. . . . I want to tell them: Don't misuse our philosophy for your own political agenda."

To illustrate, he mentioned an American working for a corporation in Bhutan who writes a blog about the country. "He recently took a picture of the only baggage carousel in the airport—and he is shocked. He is mortified to find that it's packed with flat-screen LCD television sets. About three years ago, a whole team from Brazil—Brazil is very enamored by GNH—came here. They called me for an interview. And the anchor immediately pounced on me. She said, 'We were disappointed. The airport was packed with television sets.' My answer to that lady, my answer to the American, and my answer to you is: Who on earth said Bhutan is a monastery?"

I reminded Tobgay that two eminent economists—Joseph Stiglitz, the Nobel laureate, and Jeffrey Sachs, director of the Earth Institute—have endorsed the Bhutanese example. He laughed. "I think about scholars, especially those fighting for intellectual recognition and Nobel Prizes and all that. They've got to come up with ideas. And they must be killing themselves for not coming up with Gross National Happiness. This tagline, it's so powerful."

But he was serious. "As long as the flavor of the month is not too pungent, as long as it doesn't turn off others, you can tolerate it. But the moment the livelihoods of the economists in Chicago are threatened, they will come down, and they will come down hard. So we in Bhutan must be fully aware of what's going on. It's nice to receive adulation—take it if you want it. But come back home and be real."

The ideas underlying GNH are not strictly Buddhist, he added, but could also fit into Christian, Muslim, Hindu, and other religions. "Why this Buddhist thing? Because this is also the flavor of the month," he said. "I believe in the teachings of the Lord Jesus, who said, 'The truth shall set you free.'"

I was taken aback. "Are you Buddhist or Christian?"

"Buddhist," he said. "But isn't it wonderful? 'The truth shall set you free.'"

12

Tobgay's comments were amplified during my stay in a lively debate that broke out in the daily newspaper *The Bhutanese* in September 2012. The verbal melee was sparked by a series of articles by David L. Luechauer, a former lecturer at the Royal University of Bhutan's Gaeddu College of Business Studies, now teaching at Purdue University. Lambasting what he considered the hypocrisy with which Bhutan puts its GNH ideals into practice, Luechauer provoked hundreds of online comments. For me, the debate—conducted by citizens still excited about their fledgling democracy and its unfettered market of ideas—was a window into the country's current preoccupations. Even their online handles bespoke an optimism and seriousness of purpose: goodkarma, ASimplePlan, Careful Observer, Radicalist, Bhutan 1.0.

In his first salvo, Luechauer complained that while the Bhutanese "can parrot the principles and espouse the mantra" of GNH, consumerism had them firmly in its grip. He also asserted that Bhutan was a welfare state of India, artificially buoyed by its southern neighbor's donations and cheap labor. "No India, no GNH," he wrote. (I had noticed that a popular Coca-Cola ad unwittingly played on national policy. The young woman fetchingly holding a bottle, with the slogan "Open Happiness," was an Indian model.)

With GNH, of course, Bhutan has become the hobbyhorse for evangelicals of all political stripes. It didn't take long, in subsequent columns, for Luechauer to show his true colors. "In my most contrarian moments, I sometimes wish or think that Bhutan should return to being a monarchy and that the King should follow the model Jack Welch used to save General Electric. Bhutan needs to get into the game before telling others how to play the game and right now, Bhutan isn't even in the stadium."

The following week, Luechauer let fly. GNH, he wrote, "has largely become an elitist concept embraced by fundamentalist environmentalist, left wing liberals, and economists with Marxist, Socialist, Communistic leaning." A week later, the diatribe reached full throttle. "I worry that the Bhutanese people are also being falsely led to believe that all in the west is bad, that many . . . in the west are rich but 'unhappy,' and that somehow it is the pursuit or measure of GDP [gross domestic product] that is the cause of these problems," he wrote. "Here is a newsflash: we aren't all bad, we aren't all unhappy and most of the world's issues have more to do with human nature than the pursuit or measure of GDP."

Many online comments agreed with Luechauer's critique. One listed "the need[s] of the hour," from safe drinking water and quality health care to filling potholes and providing decent public toilets. Another chimed in: "If all foreign aid was cut off for one single day, we'd collapse. . . . Most of our problems have nothing to do with GDP . . . it's about the failure of people to actually demand REAL GNH!" Added another: "I am a Bhutanese and I am against establishing stalls for selling GNH in the streets of New York, London and Rio de Janeiro."

While many Bhutanese casually denigrate GNH, they rise to its defense if outsiders take exception. Most of the comments decried Luechauer's attacks with their own invective.

Said one: "He has just expressed frustrations of a poor-ethnocentric-neoliberal-xenophobic-western-ultranationalistic-blond who failed to realise his GNH."

What Luechauer perhaps failed to appreciate is that GNH must be accounted for not only in financial spreadsheets, but in experiences that don't carry a price tag. In Thimphu, I saw a small boy "walking" a coat hanger as if it were a dog, pure delight on his face. One Saturday morning as I ate breakfast on the steps of a bank, a young girl whose T-shirt read "My carbon footprint is shrinking" sat near me, singing to herself. At the movies, instead of fast-cut, car-chase, bomb-blast trailers, sedate footage of the young king and queen illuminates the screen, and everybody stands to sing the national anthem.

When I finished reading the Luechauer series, I felt like shouting: "It's not the economy, stupid." Or, "It's not *just* the economy." Easy for a comfortably fixed out-of-towner to say. But Passang Tshering, a high school teacher in the central district of Wangdue who writes a blog titled "PaSsu Diary: Journal of an Ordinary Bhutanese," seemed to agree. "Here is another guy who came all the way [from] the US and went back with additional load of unhappiness. He comes from a country where priorities are misplaced and now can't even see a single thing straight. Send this man to heaven and he will come back with complaints. Sorry Doc, you don't understand Bhutanese lives yet, you will never."

But it was a reader named Thought who for me best conveyed the contradictions of contemporary Bhutan: "It is now time that we seriously straighten out certain flaws in system such as issues of economy structure, governance and corruption and not just focus on advertising Bhutan as this non-existent shangrila of 'GNH.' Nevertheless I truly believe if there is one piece of land on this planet earth where we can make this experiment called GNH work th[e]n one of them is Bhutan." Thought ended his (or her) remarks with a jazzy riff that perfectly captured the mutual incomprehension of this cross-cultural moment: "With the blessings of our guardian deities and the blessings of the lineage of wise masters, teachers, monarchs and leaders from the past, may the light of GNH come out of the dusty shelves, cupboards, realm of intellectual speculation, macbooks, laptops, expensive seminars and conferences, colorful kabneys and shine on the darkness of modern day material and spiritual challenges. Pelden Drukpa Lhagello. Long live Bhutan."

13

བཅུ་གསུམ་

In July 2011, Bhutan introduced its first-ever resolution to the United Nations, "Happiness: towards a holistic approach to development," which was unanimously adopted by the 193 member countries. As a follow-up, the government hosted the April 2012 UN High-Level meeting, which was attended by some 600 exuberant supporters who overflowed the conference room in New York. The atmosphere was giddy, despite the pointedly sober title of the conference: "Wellbeing and Happiness: Defining a New Economic Paradigm."

Though Jigme Thinley had been spreading the word about GNH for more than a decade, this was, in a sense, the diplomatic debut of his country's exceptional mandate. To be sure, there were skeptics in the crowd. At the "working lunch," a lawyer who had served for decades at the UN sat next to me. Scanning the vast meeting room, he had noticed only three or four bona fide diplomats; most of the attendees were from NGOs, he told me, a sure sign of the conference's insignificance. Later that afternoon, during a question-and-answer session, a tweed-and-beard attendee who introduced himself as a University of London philosopher stood up and complained that, unlike the scientifically validated concept of "well-being," "happiness" was a trifling benchmark of development. "It seems to me almost a fatuous notion," he said, to nonplussed silence.

Thinley had anticipated these detractions. "I wish to submit that, contrary to what many mistakenly believe, Bhutan is not a country that has attained GNH, and it is not from a pedestal that we serve as a humble facilitator today," he said. "Like most developing nations, we are struggling with the challenge of fulfilling the basic needs of our people. What separates us, however, from most others is that we have made happiness, the most fundamental of human needs, as the goal of societal change."

The UN conference was part of a nascent "new economy movement" based on "alternative indicators of development"—alternative, that is, to the model based on limitless growth. In the United Kingdom, the new economics foundation (lowercase intentional, perhaps to economize on printer's ink) publishes the Happy Planet Index. The European Union has a "GDP and Beyond" initiative. The World Bank's Wealth Accounting and the Valuation of Ecosystem Services partnership tallies the environmental costs and benefits of green growth. The Organization for Economic Cooperation and Development's Better Life Index is touted with the statement, "There is more to life than the cold numbers of GDP and economic statistics." (Its index looks much like the domains of Bhutan's GNH model.) Brazil is trying out GNH in cities, communities, and corporations. The Seattle Area Happiness Initiative posts a Well-Being Survey on its website, and a growing number of American cities—from Baltimore, Maryland, to Somerville, Massachusetts, to Eau Claire, Wisconsin—have also nibbled at the idea. In 2012, Vermont became the first state to pass a law that calls for establishing and testing a Genuine Progress Indicator to measure the state's economic, environmental, and societal well-being; Vermont is also headquarters for the nonprofit organization GNHUSA, the motto of which is "Measure what Matters."

So what matters? Unlike GDP, these new approaches count as benefits such intangibles as volunteer and household labor, families' care for children and the elderly, storm buffering by wetlands, good roads, safe neighborhoods. They count as costs air pollution, environmental degradation, harm to human health, crime, underemployment, lost leisure time. Alternative indicators are alternative because they measure the quality as well as the quantity of the economy.

What makes the phrase "Gross National Happiness" so brilliant is that it turns the term Gross National Product on its head. GNP is the total market value of goods and services produced by the residents of a country in a given year, even if they're living abroad. (Today, most nations measure GDP, which is the total market value of goods and services produced within the borders of a country, regardless of the nationality of those who produce them.)

We measure what we value. GNH reminds us that we

can't rely on an assessment of quantity to reflect our quality of life. For the World Bank and International Monetary Fund, GDP is a standard measure of comparative well-being, used to classify nations as advanced or less developed. Yet various international surveys, from the Happy Planet Index to the UN's World Happiness Report to the Gallup Global Wellbeing poll, have shown that well-off America ranks far from the top in terms of contentment. As Thinley explained in an interview with the UN News Center, "GDP is not so much an indicator for development as a matrix for accounting." Bhutan took the novel stance that what was important was not the pace of development, but the reflective deliberation behind it. GNH turns the metrics of the material into the metrics of the spirit.

14

Karma Ura's Centre for Bhutan Studies has devised a formula that purports to boil down national happiness into a single number:

$$GNH = 1 - (H_n \times A_n)$$

where

H_n = percent of not-yet-happy people

= $1 - H_h$ or (100 − % happy people)

and

A_n = percentage of domains in which not-yet-happy people lack sufficiency

In 2010, the most recent survey, that calculation turned out to be 0.743—which means . . . well, I don't know. It did seem to contravene what one Bhutanese friend remarked: "Isn't it the simplest thing that makes you happy? Isn't it the most complex thing that doesn't make you happy?"

Around the world, happiness indexes are proliferating, but in Bhutan, the question of measuring happiness is divisive. Even Karma Tshiteem, Secretary of the Gross National Happiness Commission, disagrees with the idea of boiling down population-wide happiness into a number. "There is this misconception that, with . . . our clever index and indicators, we are trying to measure happiness." Rather, he said, Bhutan's GNH parameters should be used like the gauges on a car's dashboard, alerting leaders to problems. Others are more skeptical, insisting that measurement is a dangerous sop to the data-driven West—dangerous because, if Bhutan fails by its own unorthodox accounting, it will no longer be a credible avatar of GNH. They say that Bhutan wasn't interested in measurement until the UN and World Bank caught wind of the idea, and the country faced international pressure to come up with hard numbers.

Jigme Thinley conceded that Bhutan's hand was initially forced by outsiders. "What the modern world wanted was a system of measures, indicators quantifying everything. At first, yes, I was not very happy with this, because the pressure was on Bhutan to adopt . . . the attitude of the material world: anything that is good must be measurable. And what is measurable and quantifiable has a price to it. And then everything comes down to economics. It is making material out of something that is more aesthetic, more spiritual, something of the mind, the emotions.

"I thought it was demeaning the sublime value that human society should be pursuing. And I also worried that developing metrics could lead to pursuing what is measurable and what is quantifiable, thereby risking the possibility of leaving out what is not quantifiable—but may be far more meaningful and far more important to creating the conditions for happiness. And so, repeating the mistake that the world has been making."

I was curious why the former prime minister had changed his mind. His answer went to the heart of the issue. "Bhutan has achieved what it has, not because we had the facility of metrics," he told me. "We simply believed in the idea of happiness being the meaning and purpose of life."

In Buddhism, the Brahma Viharas—also known as the Sublime Mental Abodes—are considered means by which one cultivates wise intention and inclusive relationships to oneself and all living beings, a liberation of the heart rooted in empathy. In a sense, they are what remain when self-concern is transcended. This ennobling quartet consists of loving-kindness, compassion, sympathetic joy, and equanimity.

In Bhutan, I saw and felt these qualities in abundance, and concluded that what made Bhutan so distinctly different from any place I'd ever been was this facet of the national character. Then I remembered another name in the Buddhist canon for the Brahma Viharas. They are called the Four Immeasurables.

15

བརྒྱ་ལྔ་

Urban legends abound in Bhutan—ours, not theirs. I often heard a genial contempt for the United States. Almost every person with whom I spoke voiced a refrain, virtually in the same words, about the loneliness in American cities. The refrain was usually a variant of two sentences: "In the U.S., you could live in a building for five [ten, twenty] years and not know your neighbor across the hall." And: "In the U.S., it takes two weeks to schedule an appointment with your best friend." Burnished by repetition, these unflattering portraits have become central to Bhutanese self-definition. Rich in what Western academics have coined (almost in self-caricature) "social capital," Bhutan silhouettes itself as what the U.S. is not.

Dasho Benji, the Fourth King's cousin, is a beloved and avuncular figure, a mischievous lampooner with a wide-browed, boyish face and protruding ears. I met him at a popular burger-and-shake joint in Thimphu called The Zone. In 2008, Benji had hosted a tent at the Smithsonian Folk Festival, in Washington, DC. "There were people who would regularly come and sit in the tent, where I would be telling stories, laughing, joking. They loved it. They would come every day. I welcomed them because they must be very lonely people, and I felt sorry for them. Many of them live a lie: Their family is far away, they're in a big city, it's just going to their office, back to their little apartment, very little social life. Or they go to their local bar, spin a yarn. I draw these conclusions from a collection of anecdotes of Bhutanese who have lived in America. They would say: 'We've been here five years and we don't even know who our next-door neighbor is.'"

One afternoon, I met two young women hitchhikers, both vocational education students. When the bolder of the two learned where I was from, she informed me, in scolding, British-inflected English, "If you go back to your country, you won't want to stay." Then she asked me about life in the United States. I wanted to paint a thoughtful and nuanced picture, but I found myself gabbling about lack of leisure. Like many Americans, I rue the dearth of free time in my day— time to *do nothing.* Traveling through a place like Bhutan, the false frenzy of American life seems even more appalling. I could hear that my speech sounded rushed and frantic. Unbidden, I was dramatizing the Bhutanese stereotype about America. After a few minutes, I finally sputtered to a stop.

"Ma'am," she observed, "in your country, there is no GNH."

In his rustic office, I asked Karma Ura if he feels culture shock when he visits the U.S. "No culture shock," he assured me, explaining that the terrifying allegories that abound in Vajrayana Buddhism had prepared him for American cities. But in the U.S., he said, "Human beings look so small, so insignificant, so lost. It's just kind of a sadness." Karma Tshiteem made the same point. When he goes abroad, "The standard of living is high—hot food ready all the time, the comfort of escalators and elevators and nice buses and subways. But when you come to the quality of life, working twelve hours, four hours commute on a train, it doesn't make sense to me." In Bhutan, time never seemed hoarded. Even those in prestigious positions spoke at a leisurely pace, lingering after my recorder was turned off and continuing the conversation in e-mails once I returned home. Though I'm well aware of

Bhutanese rules of hospitality, this kindness never felt dutiful.

I asked Tshiteem what he misses about Bhutan when he is out of the country. "This is what I miss: You can't just walk up to someone and smile and say something. There is so little trust, human relations are so broken down. I sometimes joke with my colleagues, 'I would like to have this as a GNH indicator: that today, if you are a visitor in Bhutan, someone will walk up to you and start talking to you for twenty minutes—for no reason.' This is a good indicator of a flourishing society. That humanity exists, and not everything is about buying and selling and transactions. That you can have spontaneous exchanges, just because we happen to inhabit this planet and share this precious life at the same time."

16

བཙུ་དྲུག

When I mentioned that I would be interviewing Neten Zangmo, chairperson of the Anti-Corruption Commission, people often lapsed into a kind of tongue-tied heroine-worship. "There is no agenda behind her. There is no restraint in her. It's so refreshing." "She is afraid of nobody. She is a lady who is not interested in material pursuit." "She is our nation's only tigress." In 2008 the king bestowed on Zangmo the Red Scarf—one of the highest honors a Bhutanese civilian can receive, for outstanding service to the nation—"for carrying out her duties as head of the ACC without fear or favour."

The commission has conducted investigations into illegal land transfers, misdeeds in the mining industry, political corruption, questionable procurements, bribery in hydroelectric projects. Members also ventured to a remote, 35-household village to probe the politically motivated government distribution of 14 cows.

When I was in Bhutan, the headlines were dominated by a land scandal being investigated by the ACC. A decade earlier, plots in Gyelpozhing town and nearby areas in the east had been illegally allotted. Violating decrees from the king, high government ministers, judges, senior bureaucrats, members of the royal family, and others took or accepted land meant for farmers and shopkeepers who had lost their properties when a hydroelectric project and secondary school were built. As ACC chair, Zangmo was leading the charge.

Her headquarters occupy the top floor of a new office building in Thimphu, where just a few feet from the entrance one sees a decrepit chorten, one of the innumerable squat monuments dotting the landscape that are built to protect a place against evil spirits. The old chorten stood on an ancient footpath, and Zangmo, overruling the architect, refused to move the sacred but inconveniently situated shrine. She had once told a reporter that as a child, she rolled up her sleeves to challenge boys in her class. "I am trying to be a Boddhisattva warrior," she said. "Trying to free myself from the worldly dharma, trying to cultivate 'I-could-not-care-less attitude.'"

Zangmo is charismatic: upbeat, direct, self-deprecating, without pretense. Her dark hair is cut short, her wire-rim glasses are cool, and her red-and-white version of the traditional full *kira*—a fussy garment that can appear dowdy and restrictive—had clean and relaxed lines. An engineer by training, "I'm not a philosopher," she said, "so you will not hear high-flung things from me. GNH, to me, is basically a fulfilling of my responsibility—sincerely serving the people, actually earning my salary."

In Bhutan—a country where everybody knows everybody—nepotism and conflict of interest are the most common issues under Zangmo's purview. The Bhutanese complain of "phone call syndrome," where people with the right family and professional connections can vault ahead of others in line for a job or other competitive position. "Gift giving was a part of the culture. But now we are seeing that this subtle dimension of bribery—seeking for favors—is also there," she explained. "People say that we are undermining our traditions. But we are saying, 'What is your intention of giving the gift?' When you talk about corruption, it's the intention."

"But isn't corruption endemic in human nature?" I asked.

Zangmo replied that the ACC wasn't interested only in exposing crime and putting people behind bars. It was also engaged in educating youth to be spiritually self-aware. "Citizens will have to reflect on the sort of society we're creating, the character of the nation, and what kids think about honesty, especially in relating to oneself. If I see somebody doing wrong, will I report it?"

With materialism, she added, "We have reached a very vulnerable stage." The 2012 Bhutan Living Standards Survey found that the mean income of the richest consumption quintile was more than five times that of the poorest consumption quintile—not bad by U.S. standards, but a yawning gap for an erstwhile subsistence culture like Bhutan's, even with its small but enduring class of moneyed landowners. Zangmo worries that rising wealth will contaminate, American-style, Bhutan's tender democracy. "This is one of my biggest fears—the gap between the rich and the poor. The rich are getting richer, and policies are designed to cater to the needs of the people who give you money for your campaigning . . . they're almost like your shadow policymakers. When you look around you, so much conflict, so much suffering, so much distrust, wealth being concentrated on a few people, the environment being plundered. This we can't afford to have in Bhutan, because we are fragile in every way: socially, environmentally, politically."

17

In Buddhism, each of the Brahma Viharas—the Sublime Mental Abodes—has a "far enemy" and a "near enemy." The far enemy is the virtuous mind's polar opposite—cruelty is the far enemy of compassion, for example. But the near enemy of these optimal states is trickier to recognize and root out, because while it seems to be wholesome, it is tinged with "mental poisons," or destructive emotions. The near enemy of compassion, for instance, is pity.

Traveling through Bhutan, a country that pierced me with kindness, I kept thinking of the concept of near enemy. To my mind, the near enemy of Bhutan's generosity and self-acceptance and abundant sense of time is complacency. My own examples were petty: dangerous holes that went unrepaired in the street near my hotel, fatalistic replies when I would ask about construction codes or sanitation standards in the expanding capital, a sense that people often take the easy solution rather than the effective one. Many of my contacts there also seemed disquieted by this shadow side of their benign culture. As a reader observed in *The Bhutanese,* "The truth is that GNH or no GNH we still struggle with our daily problems of corruption, indifference and our general tendency to slack away at everything we do and give it the name of GNH."

One acquaintance put a positive spin on this lack of urgency. "In terms of problems, we have patience. And sometimes, problems turn out all right in the end." For example, he said, "Holes in the road may prevent speeding." In the land of the laid-back, I often felt driven, and my American determination was—well, foreign to my hosts. I left Bhutan exhausted and vaguely aware that, in my obsessive reportorial productiveness, I had somehow, in that easy-going country, missed the boat.

To be sure, rural life in Bhutan, as in most developing nations, entails staggering hardship. The country's most unstinting workers, and those with the least sense of privilege, are surely its farmers. But elsewhere in the past 40 years, as the provisions of Gross National Happiness took hold—free health care, free education, and, for many urban dwellers, an assurance of a cushy government job—something happened. Until recently, the Royal Civil Service was the largest employer of the educated, and these undemanding office jobs were coveted. Despite a religion steeped in the idea of impermanence, citified Bhutanese had come to rely on the permanence of government employment and other benefits. Now, however, government payrolls can no longer accommodate new college graduates. "We have been spoiled," one official told me. Or as a long-term expatriate here explained, "The people have been infantilized. There is a sense of entitlement that is a time bomb for society."

Bhutanese also proudly abjure blue-collar work. In the construction sites that dominate the urban landscape, it is almost entirely Indians who hammer and saw, pour cement and lug rebar. And it is mostly Indians and Nepalese who make up the road crews that labor in broiling sun and biting cold with crude hand tools, repairing the damage from landslides.

"There are plenty of jobs, but the graduates don't want to take them because they think the job is low for them," a teenage boy told me. "They want to achieve greatness at a single step. They want to go to office carrying briefcases and laptops. They see people carrying iPhones and they want to carry them, too." Then his well-memorized GNH lessons kicked in. "Maybe they should know that if they are happy with the job, if they're contented with it, then in that way they can achieve happiness. If you do the work sincerely, who knows? You may get a promotion and an iPhone."

Ambition is an uneasy concept here. At a dinner party, I spoke with a young woman undergraduate from a prestigious women's college in the U.S.—the kind of school with a mission of nurturing self-esteem and competence, and where the word "feminism" would not feel uncomfortable. At first, she said, she couldn't get used to the speed of life in the United States. Now she's not only used to it, but feels more "ambitious" for herself. "When I come back to Bhutan, I want more," she told me.

"Is ambition good or bad?" I asked, expecting her to endorse it.

"Bad," she said, frowning. "Because it means I am discontent and always want more." Was she parroting the GNH line, or did she mean it?

18

བཅུ་བརྒྱད་

Literally and figuratively, the Bhutanese let sleeping dogs lie. But that is starting to change. The country is ringing with fresh voices. While in 2000 there was one newspaper in the country—the government-run *Kuensel*—today there are 12, though nearly all are struggling to survive on low ad revenue. More than 84,000 Bhutanese are on Facebook and 5,000 on Twitter. Lively blogs command thousands of followers. And GNH is jokingly said to stand for Gross National Haranguing or Gross National Harassment.

Having newly found their voices, some Bhutanese have conceived an admiration for the U.S., which they perceive as culturally more upfront. This is especially true of those who have lived in the States. "What I liked about people there is they don't have a double standard," said Chimi Wangmo, the feminist who directs the anti–domestic violence group RENEW—which stands for Respect, Educate, Nurture and Empower Women. "They are who they are. And because they are very forthright, if they do not like something, they will just say it. And if they do like it, they will also say it. Bhutanese people have a double standard: They say one thing and mean another."

As Wangmo knows well, domestic violence has been shrouded in silence. Bhutan's 2010 Multiple Indicator Survey found that 68.4 percent of women ages 15 to 49 "believed that a man was justified in hitting or beating his wife if the woman was not respecting the 'family norms' such as going out without telling a husband, neglecting a child, burning the food or refusing to have sex with him." When she began lobbying lawmakers for a bill banning domestic violence, Wangmo was met with incredulity. Opponents insisted that there couldn't be domestic violence in Bhutan, because "Bhutan is a GNH nation." She countered their tautologies with facts, inviting legislators to RENEW's headquarters to view photographs and videos of battered women. (In February 2013, the National Council passed the Domestic Violence Prevention Bill.)

"Bhutan must come out of self-denial: It is not a Shangri-la," said Wangmo. "No matter how much we flaunt GNH, no matter how much we picture ourselves as a happiness country, the hard reality remains that we are among the most backward, poorest countries in the world. GNH is a beautiful concept. But we could do better than this—not just talking about GNH, but living it. It's basically fundamental human rights, which the Western countries have done much, much better than us."

In the land of GNH, the doctrine of human rights is not deeply ingrained. In my conversations, I noticed that faces turned blank when I broached the subject of Nepalese refugees from southern Bhutan—an issue that seems more conversationally alive in the West than in Bhutan itself, though the matter is far more complex than the distillation I had heard back home. Starting in the 1960s, thousands of laborers of Nepalese origin came here to build roads and work on other infrastructure projects. Economic migrants also slipped into the country through its open southern borders. In 1988, when Bhutanese officials ordered a census and embarked on other measures to curb illegal immigration and a growing antigovernment movement, there was violence on both sides and tens of thousands of people of Nepali origin either fled or were expelled, mostly to camps in eastern Nepal. Few of my acquaintances knew what I was talking about, or cared. As one young woman said, "We never learned about it in school."

I visited Motithang Higher Secondary School one morning to talk to teenagers—a group I assumed would be brimming with unvarnished opinions. Signs in the hallway attested to the spirit of freethinking. "The Ink of the Scholar Is More Sacred Than the Blood of Martyr," read one. "If you have inner peace nobody can force you to be a slave to outer reality," exhorted another. Yet when I met with a group of older students, I was struck by their conservatism and bland recitation of GNH rhetoric. This style of erudition is partly sown by a hierarchical British education model, where there is typically one right answer, critical thinking is seldom encouraged, and teachers are revered—or in any case, not to be defied. Still, I couldn't help notice that the boys held forth with confidence and smoothness, even a bit of arrogance, while the girls hung back and smiled. The dynamics felt demoralizingly familiar, my own high school experience all over again.

"What if Bhutan isn't Bhutan one day?" asked one young man. His question wasn't really a question, but a preamble. "What people like about Bhutan—the reason why tourists come to Bhutan—is because we have one culture. We don't really mix it with other countries. Because if we do, then slowly at first, it's maybe three-fourths Bhutan, one-fourth Korea. Then after a while, it becomes half Korea, half Bhutan. Then three-fourths of Korea. And then one day, Bhutan is Korea. Maybe we don't want that. We want Bhutan to be Bhutan." And so it went. I couldn't tell if the conversation was rote or real.

Toward the end, a young woman named Sonam finally spoke up, and the air in the room quickly became charged. "Dare I say it? I want to be a writer," she said. "I want to be a writer and I want to go into detail on how a life is for a woman who has faced violence and how a life is for a prostitute girl. People won't accept it if I talk openly about it—they will say, 'She's a bit of a loose character, talking to prostitutes and all.' Or if I go out with a gangster because I want to know his life, they will say, 'She goes out with a gangster.' Me being a girl, doing this stuff, it might not be accepted. But it's what I love to do, you know?"

19

བཙུ་དགུ་

"There are only seven hundred thousand of us," one man told me. "And here we are between India and China. If we were an animal, we would be on the endangered species list."

On July 13, 2013, voters in the land of Gross National Happiness expressed startling unhappiness with their ruling party. In the country's second national election, citizens chose the pro-business, small-government People's Democratic Party, vaulting the outspoken former opposition leader in Parliament, Tshering Tobgay, into the post of prime minister. Although his vision of the role of government is diametrically opposite that of the previous regime, Tobgay has not repudiated GNH—he just wants it to work better.

Bhutan is at a delicate inflection point, poised between centuries-long traditions and an understandable rush toward material security and the myriad things the affluent West takes for granted (including, it must be said, things like safe roads and proficient medical care, which all governments owe their citizens). Will these ambitions subvert or undo the poetic possibilities of GNH? The psychiatrist Chencho Dorji fears that while the quality of life in Bhutan's fast-growing urban areas may improve in the short term, after a few generations it will sour—in part because the deep social connections forged by rural nonmoney culture will fade away. "Certainly, there are good reasons for rural people to say they are happier in town," he said. "In town, you get three, four square meals a day, the bar is just next door, the school is around the corner, water is in the house, the hospital is free, you don't have to walk three or ten miles to find a doctor or health worker."

The list sounded pretty good to me. I wondered if he was romanticizing rural adversity. "But we have to complete the cycle," he continued. "In the rural setup, you don't need money: you can borrow, you can barter, you can beg. Your values are not tied to money. In an urban place, everything is dependent on money. And when everything is monetized, that is the source of greed and selfishness."

Lama Ngodup put a dharma spin on the shifting era. "In a materialistic world, impermanence is rather ignored. And when you think everything is permanent, the game turns out to be a risky field." Ngodup happened to be in the Berkshires on the morning of 9/11. For him, the attacks underscored the necessity of reflecting upon transience—and cherishing life. "GNH becomes more possible when impermanence is taken seriously."

One morning, I sat by the big front window of the Ambient Café with the author Kunzang Choden. Her 2005 book, *The Circle of Karma,* was the first novel by a Bhutanese woman. Written in English, it is the story of Tsomo, a protagonist cruelly propelled from one holy place to another, seemingly by karma, until she finally abandons all attachments. "Think of all the choices that a solitary and unattached pilgrim has. Choose wisely," Tsomo is presciently advised early on in the story. On a grand historical scale, Bhutan has also been a solitary pilgrim.

"I often read things like, 'This cannot happen in a GNH country,'" Choden said, referring to lawmakers' postured disbelief when social problems are covered in the media. "But a GNH country is also made up of human beings, so anything can happen." Soft-spoken and refined, in a dark green *kira* and mauve scarf, she listed Bhutan's emerging realities: "youth unemployment, delinquency, alcoholism, drug abuse, children born out of wedlock, single mothers, and we also have groups of people who are affected with HIV and AIDS."

I asked Choden what Bhutan's circle of karma looks like. "Karma is not fatalism. Karma can be regulated. You can change karma, and the change begins with you," she explained. "I believe in the cumulative merits and demerits of all the people, as a nation. And I think Bhutan's future is going to be the outcomes of all the cumulative merits and demerits of the people of this generation. Which way it goes, I cannot say."

While preparing for my trip, I had read a number of blogs from Bhutan. One in particular struck me as eloquent, authored by someone who deeply understood this cultural turning point. "Land of the Thunder Dragon" is written by Yeshey Dorji, a government bureaucrat-turned entrepreneur-turned-nature-photographer. I had e-mailed him months earlier to ask for an interview in Thimphu. Our initially formal correspondence turned into a lively exchange.

I finally met him on the street in front of my hotel in Thimphu. Tall and bespectacled, dressed in jeans and a black quilted Patagonia jacket, he was gracious, impatient, cantankerous, and funny as hell. Everyone seemed to know and respect him. Wherever we went in Thimphu, people greeted him with a smile or came up to talk politics or gossip, and I thought of him as the unofficial mayor. One day I asked him, "What are you in this country? Are you a gadfly? A contrarian?" He laughed. "No. See, Madeline, I love my country. If Bhutan should go down, I would be nothing."

Dorji is highly attuned to the poignancy of impending loss. "We have jumped from one very strange period to another very strange period," he explained. "Today, people have all the time in the world to talk to you. It's not productive, but it's the human side of life. Soon, development will change all that. Bhutanese people will be abrupt, fast-moving. They will no longer be Bhutanese."

Yet he also believes that Bhutan could learn from the American example. "Times have changed. We have to change ourselves. But we aren't willing to do that. I am convinced the Bhutanese mentality needs a makeover—total. We keep complaining about how fast your life is in New York. But without the development of that culture, you wouldn't be where you are." He visited the U.S. in the 1980s, and even finagled his way into Studio 54, the storied New York nightclub. "That was *the* place to be!" he said gleefully. What he admires about American culture are its energy, innovation, drive, curiosity, cosmopolitanism, ambition—qualities, in fact, that are conspicuous in Dorji himself, and have enabled him to be a shrewd observer/participant in his homeland.

Like many people I met here, Dorji feels caught between two ideals: the past perfect and the future perfect. "Development changes the way people move, talk, think, the way they look at value. If you keep the same old habits, then you can't change the Bhutanese," he said. "But the moment you change the Bhutanese, you've probably lost GNH."

20

Why did the concept of Gross National Happiness spring up in Bhutan? Because of an inspired monarch, uncommon political unity, and what many refer to as a "splendid isolation" that enabled policymakers to learn from other nations' mistakes. But mostly because it is almost impossible to separate Bhutanese culture from the spiritual riches of Buddhism. Bhutan was a GNH country before there was GNH.

In Gross National Happiness, Bhutan has cultivated an idealistic self-image that is about to shatter. Yet my travels here convinced me that, despite its flaws and self-delusions—no more or less than any other country—Bhutan has much to teach Americans, even if we don't quite recognize it. I think of Apple Computers co-founder Steve Jobs, who, singing the psalm of consumerism, famously said: "People don't know what they want until you show it to them."

That modern truism flows in both directions. Today, the wealthy world is showing Bhutan not only what it doesn't know it wants, but also what it doesn't know it eventually *won't* want: the gluttony and waste, electronic distraction and social anomie, earbuds and diabetes, frantic schedules and regrets for lost time, the too-muchness of what doesn't matter and the not-enoughness of what does. Boastful of having never been colonized by an outside power, Bhutan is being insidiously overtaken, not exactly by greed, as the official line goes, but by false need.

In Buddhist parlance, the country is drifting in *bardo*, the intermediate state between death and rebirth. A famous masked dance dramatizes this transition by vividly depicting peaceful and wrathful deities, so that audience members will recognize these antagonistic creatures when they meet them again after death. Gazes are riveted on the sacred spectacle— I'd never seen such rapt concentration—because viewing the dance is believed to free one from rebirth in lower realms. In the Buddhist tradition, learning through images is considered more potent than learning through reason. The Buddha, after all, could only show the way.

As their splendid isolation expires, will Bhutanese recognize what's at stake for them—but not only for them? If they collectively find a wise path, will the rest of the world learn by observing the tiny kingdom's leap of imagination? Will Bhutan's 1.0 be the template for our 2.0? Does humanity even get a 2.0?

Unlikely. But I long to return and witness the experiment.

བཀྲིས་བདེ་ལེགས།།

Acknowledgments

I am grateful to my friends, colleagues and sources who made this essay possible with their insights and practical advice.

In the U.S. and Canada, I am obliged to Alejandro Adler, Gloria Taraniya Ambrosia, Lhakpa Bhuti, Bruce Bunting, Ron Colman, John de Graaf, Lore Detenber, Cynthia Enloe, Jane Friedman, Dan Gilbert, Billy Giraldi, Adam Goldberg, Carey Goldberg, Jon Greenberg, Amy Gutman, Sam Harp, John Helliwell, Ben Kerman, Daphne Mazuz, Paula McCree, Kathy Morley, Mike Morley, Tenzin Nyinjee, Martha Pennock, Michael Pennock, Ajahn Punnadhammo, Sara Rimer, Connie Rosemont, Larry Rosenberg, Joni Seager, Dawa Sherpa, Alejandro Souza, Danielle Stevenson, and Michael Voligny. I thank Alicia Doyon for the beautiful cover and text design. For their incisive comments on various drafts, I owe a particular debt of gratitude to Rick Fleeter, EJ Graff, Melissa Ludtke, X Bonnie Woods, and Laura Zimmerman. And I am immensely grateful to Chris Jerome for her encouragement and editorial guidance.

In Bhutan, I thank Upasana Dahal, Atti-La Dahlgren, Kezang Dema, Chencho Dorjee, Gampo Dorji, Tandin Gyeltshen, Gepke Hingst, Randall Krantz, Françoise Pommaret, Lily Wangchuk, Sonam Wangda, Lenny Zangmo, and the folks at the Ambient Café. I can't begin to express my appreciation to Yeshey Dorji—gifted writer and nature photographer, and a true citizen of Bhutan—whose generosity opened so many doors. Finally, I am beholden to the many individuals in Bhutan who patiently answered my questions and made me feel welcome in their country.

About the Author

Madeline Drexler is an award-winning journalist, author, and travel essayist. She is editor of *Harvard Public Health* magazine and a senior fellow at Brandeis University's Schuster Institute for Investigative Journalism. Among her national honors: selected for *Best American Travel Writing 2015* (Houghton Mifflin Harcourt); 2015 Finalist, Next Generation Indie Book Awards; 2014 Grand Gold Winner for Best Article of the Year, CASE Circle of Excellence Awards; 2012 Sigma Delta Chi Award for Public Service in Magazine Journalism; 2012 Clarion Award for Feature Articles; and 1996-1997 Knight Science Journalism Fellowship at MIT. Drexler's articles have appeared in *The New York Times, The Wall Street Journal, The Nation, The American Prospect, The New Republic, Tricycle, The Los Angeles Times, The Boston Globe, Nieman Reports, Good Housekeeping,* and many other national publications. Her book *Emerging Epidemics: The Menace of New Infections* (Penguin, 2010), originally issued in 2003 as *Secret Agents: The Menace of Emerging Infections,* drew wide critical praise. Drexler began her career as a staff photographer for The Associated Press.

For more information on Madeline Drexler's writing and photography, go to www.madelinedrexler.com.

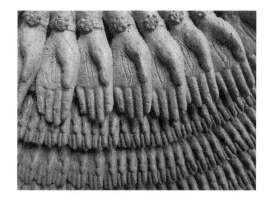

Made in the USA
San Bernardino, CA
30 January 2019